DIVINE PERFECTION

poetry *pt* today

Divine Perfection

Edited by
Rebecca Mee

First published in Great Britain in 1999 by Poetry
Today, an imprint of
Penhaligon Page Ltd, 12 Godric Square, Maxwell Road,
Peterborough. PE2 7JJ

A Catalogue record for this book is available from the
British Library

ISBN 1 86226 576 3

Typesetting and layout, Penhaligon Page Ltd, England
Printed and bound by Forward Press Ltd, England

Foreword

Divine Perfection is a compilation of poetry, featuring some of our finest poets. This book gives an insight into the essence of modern living and deals with the reality of life today. We think we have created an anthology with a universal appeal.

There are many technical aspects to the writing of poetry and *Divine Perfection* contains free verse and examples of more structured work from a wealth of talented poets.

Poetry is a coat of many colours. Today's poets write in a limitless array of styles: traditional rhyming poetry is as alive and kicking today as modern free-verse. Language ranges from easily accessible to intricate and elusive.

Poems have a lot to offer in our fast-paced 'instant' world. Reading poems gives us an opportunity to sit back and explore ourselves and the world around us.

Contents

A Hug For Diana - RIP

(From an admirer who has tears in her heart, in her eyes and in her soul)

She's still here
with
us.

We, her great British public.

She was our Princess
of the people
and of our hearts.

She's here with us,
with the ducks
as they wag their tails
and feast gluttonously on the wealth of duckweed.

She's here with us
as the petunias blow gently
to and fro,
cascading from their baskets,
as colourful as you were, Diana.

She's here with us
in peace
and in solace
and serene, at last.
God knows, you deserve it, Diana.
Like your friends
for whom you defied public ignorance
and shook hands without gloves
God knows, you said, they deserve a hug.

So this is my hug to you.

And
I
will
not
forget
the
31st August, 1997
the day that you were sent to your own Dodi happy heaven.

Cath Simpkins

The Gull

The soaring gull swoops over and down the roof,
White with sun gilded wings,
Gliding past my window, shuts me in.
Trapped by a seagull in the suburban terrace.

I hear the sound of the green, glittering,
Tumbling sea. Foam flying,
So very far away. But there before my eye
Topped by the wind, the hissing spray sighs back in.

Wafted by the gull's wing from the blue sky
Down upon the red roof,
Down into the street below, below my feet
On the throbbing deck of the sea-cutting ship.

The wind cleaves the sparkling air as sharp as
The cry of the planing gull
Widening the world as its echoes spread,
Carried down the speeding wind.

I look at the horizon, seeking the deep
Blue placid ocean,
Swelling with immense strength, gently
Unstoppable, swinging masts between the stars.

Soughing funnels breathe and dip.
The moon, magical
And majestic, floods the world with light
That holds me there forever, upon the wooden deck.

In a moment the gull has left my view.
The rolling waves
Have left the street, dry, as quickly as they came.
Only the rhythmic echo remains to trouble me.

Still in my mind, I sail the green sea,
The salt filled wake
Marks my path across the world, towards
Blue oceans and a never ending voyage,

Where the deep lark of space, turned blue by sun,
Reflects itself in the ocean
And no horizon can be seen. Where stars sit on
The masthead and the moon enchants me still.

J J S Clare

Requiem For Summer

In the goe-hairst the wyle-guse flees,
In the goe-hairst the wyle-guse cries,
In the goe-hairst, frost-rin' dichts the trees,
Comes the goe-hairst, simmer dies.

Remember, oh, remember
late October days:
beeches radiant in their russet robes;
still air, crisp and cool in autumn sunshine:
echoing summer past,
verging on winter chill.

As the lingering afternoon light
begins to fade,
on soft, inexorable pinions
winter's heralds come.

A faint, delicate, barely audible fluting
turns eager eyes westwards
for that first glimpse
of the grey geese coming.

Their song fills the twilight
as the endless skeins surge ever larger,
arrow-sharp with purpose,
across the darkening sky,
their poignant voices merging
in requiem for the summer's passing.

We stand, entranced,
while the grey geese pass,
watching, in half a melancholy hour,
the autumn day and autumn die together.

The dark sky empties, the chorale fades
as frost-sharp stars appear;
the geese float down to ground to rest,
and we, reflective in sadness,
slip inside to think of winter.

goe-hairst the period between the end of harvest and the
      beginning of winter

Ken Angus

The Beech Tree

Paint me a beech tree
In February?
It's grey!
Grey stout trunk
- Go look.
Paint me a beech tree
In sudden sun?
Vibrant emerald,
Glowing moss.
Paint me a beech tree
Cloud grey?
Sun green?

Elizabeth Gwilliam

Lines On A Crippled Bird

Brief bird upon my hand,
heart fast beating,
warming, fleeting,
fearful to start or to stand.
What banquet of days have you planned for,
what skies to rifle with song,
riding the heaven's high land?

'I rode no wind
or planned a far-flung banquet
caught at this moment
in your hand.
No land I craved for
save the seasons' land,
wreathed worm or crawling insect,
a crumb of comfort in my thorn-edged nest,
an ease from labour,
three summers and three winters spanned
before eternal rest.'

I placed the bird on sand,
crippled wing outstretched,
bright beady eye undimmed
reflecting sea and strand,
so much purpose crammed
into so small a compass,
taking its leave of life
in scarlet breast.

R Ford

Untitled

The great sea swirl, that poisoned air,
mist dark, green and foreboding where,
along the sea's edge, crustaceans live.
Live limpet to the rock ekes out
existence from primeval days to this
by sifting shifting sands for meat.

The rock looms large.
Behind, dark shadows.
Grains of sand fly into the dunes' darkness.

Moist air, comfortless and salty
lurks around round pebbles.
Pink pebbles left too long,
then battered, sculpted to new forms.

Invisible the new forms
disappearing backward into light.

Iona Doniach

A Noble Tree

O noble tree
Proud and steadfast on the hill-top
Branches waving in the morning breeze
A home, a refuge, to large and small
Lying naked in the winter sun
Exposed for all to see.
Your secret home has been
Ravaged by wind and rain.
As spring beckons, your
Protective mantle holds within its bosom
The cycle of life and their security
Is assured.

Jim Bennett

Saqqara Garden At Dusk

In the dusty dusk the garden shimmers.
The last heat of the day dies out.
The rising moon washes the garden with silver, bleaching already
faded colours.
In the quiet dark insects chirrup their last.
Palms, monochrome stir in the breeze.
Whilst in the valley
lights bejewel the dark.
The desert dogs howl whilst the heady scent of jasmine
floats sickly sweet, embalming the night.
Pale, ghostly moths as big as hands
flit and vanish like the souls of dead kings.
The screen door slaps shut,
clattering, rattling breaking the stillness.
Light floods the terrace bringing chatter,
the smell of food.
Gin glasses clink invitingly.
The high sky canopy as black as a tomb,
pinpricked with brilliants, envelopes the garden.
Ancient stillness fills the necropolis.
Ancient sepulchres bulk in the gathering dark,
huddle together, exhaling warmth gathered from the daylight.
Arabic blazes across the quiet
then fades with the sun.
The garden sighs in blessed cool.

Sally Swain

The Winter Trees

I see a tree, winter-bare,
Its scarecrow branches
Black against a steely sky,
Forlorn and stripped of beauty.
Yet still it has a striking dignity.
I sense the glory that lies hidden there,
Disguised by shabby bark and bony branches.
I love the winter trees that stand
Etched against a scowling sky.
They promise beauty soon to come,
Yet some just see a tree.

Eileen Green

You May Break A Bud

You may break a bud
from the parent stem;
you may peel back the sepals
to reveal the promise of beauty;
you may unfold the tender petals
until the heart is laid bare;
but you cannot make it blossom
or release its fragrance
and a bud so treated
can only die.

Jean Collins

The Garden

The garden shines with all its beauty.
Its harvest of golden produce adorns the silent table.
I see mother nature in all her splendour
Adorn her majestic path.

The spider gingerly weaves her silken thread
Across the succulent new green heather.
There hidden amongst the darkness she waits,
Beneath her beautiful woven deadly masterpiece
For her innocent victim.
Unbeknown to her, she is also a victim.

W G Cresswell

Lakeside Rendezvous

Creeping willow limbs extend,
frosted sliver ripples waver
beneath,
a touch timid,
delicate tendrils dip,
enchanted affectionate ripples
swathe,
cool the breeze strokes,
the willow bows,
gentle limbs ascend contented,
tenacious water resides to
waiver rippling on.

T A Peachey

The Comet

Hail thee mysterious body
Hale-Bopp riding the midnight sky
Watched by a hundred million eyes,
Uniquely regulated,
By seconds over a thousand years
Both travellers in space,
Both tickets issued by the master,
Join us with greetings
Both on track
Both on time
But are you sure
We have doubts,
We may have lost the way.

J Walbeoffe-Wilson

Music Of Light

The winter trees are filled with sun -
   has the fog flowered?
where has the cobwebby fog gone?

Under an oak I find a world
   like a nebula.
A grizzled frame has filled with gold -

I look up, listen; umber lanes
   twist with liquid flames;
it's music! My eyes fill with tunes

That haunt the weeping hush of woods
   with a brindled prism
of melisma; it's an aubade's

dominion in microcosm.

Chris White

Cat

I love thee, O Cat,
For achieving unity between the realities and the trivialities
    of life; for retaining regality when discovered indulging
    in a fish-entangled dream of cream with whisker-twitching
    anticipation.
I love thee, O Cat,
For the height of the lithe lightness that leaps to the
    inconsequential feather; for the depth of the deep
    contemplation that muses on the hidden truth buried in the
    huge universe; for the breadth of the untouchable serenity
    of feline peace.
I love thee, O Cat,
For thy perfection in a world imperfect which makes thee not a
    lover but Love, not a hunter but Fate, not a killer but
    Death itself.
Because I have loved with Love and fought with Fate and am
    doomed to Death,
I love thee, O Cat.

Catherine Gregory

Sunset

The sky is bright with the glow of the
  setting sun,
birds fly swiftly to their nests, one by one.
Trees are silhouetted black against the sky,
as the sun sinks ever lower, like a big
  golden eye.

Watch the fast changing colours,
yellow, gold and red, as the sun wallows
ever deeper into the horizon,
until it sleeps and is gone.

    Joyce G Shinn

Black Cat

Black cat sits in the window.
Staring down the road.
Silently, statuesque.
Staring down the road.
Ears prick.
Tail curls.
Ears twitch.
Black cat sits expectantly.
Watching and waiting.
Finally, deflating into an irregular fur shape of purrfection.

Pat Fewings

Changing Seasons

Hazy light, shining moon
Laced with cotton cloud
Black velvet skies
Diamonds, scattered stars
Spring arriving

Warm red glowing embers
Beautiful sun set
Burning the horizon
Long summer nights lingering

Soft gentle breeze blowing
Colour changing trees
Moon shadowed Sun
Autumn's eve

Bright, white, blue skies
Laden with snow
Fresh, freeze and chill
Winter, is here

Lorraine Elizabeth Chaytor

Cotswold Village

The charms of the village are mainly these -
the winter light through the naked trees,
the twisting paths and wandering ways
through the random labyrinthine maze
that runs uphill from the brook below
to the houses we call America Row,
the nameless pitches that surround
the cottage grown up from the ground,
(for man has worked with Nature here
through many a hungry Cotswold year),
the clear cold streams from hidden springs
running by walls where the ivy clings,
the friendly word at the garden gate,
the curling smoke from the log-filled grate,
the wide sky, gold in the evening sun,
and the Severn-bound gulls when the day is done.
Again the trees in their summer dress
framing the meadows with loveliness
and, guarding us all, our silent shield
the Church standing over the barleyfield.

Alfred Leeding

Faith

My dog Bolivar
Taught me to be faithful to God
He followed me everywhere
He was a beautiful Lassie collie
A stray

He taught me to be gentle and to be good
And kind and thoughtful
But this dog's faith in me to feed him
Every day and brush him . . .
Or no one would

In return Bolivar would protect me
And wait for me when I returned from school
He would play with me and love me
When ever I was lonely or sad
He would come

He was the colour of buttercups and dandelions
That God created for us
Bolivar would howl for me in the early hours
And look for me in ears of growing yellow corn
Yes he would find me

Climbing out of bed and out the window
Calling for him with his yellow plastic bowl of food
And another full of clear blue water
And Bolivar would drink and eat and drink again
Thank me with a swish of tail

Then winter came
We would go to church
But the tune of Christmas carols
Be ringing in our ears
In one particular
'O come all you faithful'

Would be Bolivar's tune to me.

Juel Crake

Migraine

We feel that dull, returning ache,
Knowing that soon, our heads will partake,
Of feelings, one cannot express
Loneliness, darkness, complete repress
Close that curtain, the light contain,
From burning eyes, searing pain
Lying with mind's bursting and tight,
Giving impressions of hopelessness.
Here once again that murderous rite
How to retain one's sanity
When pains so intense, it's not vanity
To wish for tomorrow, come quickly now
Please Lord, remember, those suffering
So. And give some unburdening softening
Lift a soul bereft, with thoughts of calm
Instil into beings that need to rearm
To draw back the drapes, feel new life
Has entered the chamber of sickness and strife.
Mind's clearing, seeing new light,
Expressions of gladness, recovery made,
We need God's help.
        From that fearful shade.

Albert Boddison

Prayer

I hope the world's a little wiser
The sky's a little brighter
For all that I have passed by
I hope a smile's a little clearer
A laugh's a little louder
And all the tears I see are wiped dry

Richard Lecrivain

Spending Spree

In line abreast on shelves all around,
Every kind of food is found,
Take a basket help yourself, tinned fish is cheap,
All the goods displayed are so cheap,
Attracted by baits of cash and reductions,
Housewives flock in and go rash,
They buy all kinds of food in sight,
That tempt them from shelves dazzling bright,
Gorgonzola cheese, large bags of frozen peas,
Jars of pickled onions Chutney green,
Two dozen eggs and ham and bacon lean,
Music blares tunes making such a clatter,
How much now? It does seem to matter,
No one warns her of her folly,
As she speeds along, with piled up trolley,
Now she's waiting in the queue,
Standing to pay her due, Day of wrath!
O doom impending, all good things have an ending,
Looking at the large account,
From the machine taped accounts,
The poor housewife pales and fears,
When her shopping bill she sees,
Sweet music is heard no more,
From this large and dazzling store,
Only the truth of one mad spree,
That, what is bought, is also not free.

William G Whalley

Love No More

You cannot hold me
Nor your arms enfold me
With my spirit flying,
While our love lies dying.

Helen Hazelerigg

Volcano

This inward turbulence of earth's element overheating
Hear Vulcan's drum and cymbal beating
Cataclysmic music keeps repeating
To the bubble and boil deep below earth's rock and soil
Tempo pulsating stewing waiting
Gas expanding constant pressure, searching every crack and
fissure.
Explosive waiting to give vent
And so break free from earth's restrained intent
With strident sound like devils trumpet blast and hellish bang
Larva and debris skyward go, ash laden clouds overhang.
Smoking, sulphur choking blood red river's flow
A magna slide to creep and glide
Searing shimmering heat of lava tide
Earth's crucible its destructive contents pouring
Rocks as missiles skyward soaring.
Nought can against this power prevail
Like prehistoric earth's first spawning and its birth travail
And then as now as volcanic wrath is stirred
Resounding vulcanian music as originally scored,
Once more is heard

R Powell

Friendship

Spring of friendship bubbles forth
Amid the mountains high
Draped within the clouds of life
Clouds of life float by
Stream across the boulders strewn
Hands across they touch
Friendship grows with every moon
Upon its worldly crutch
Until the lowlands creep a brook
No hand can touch from side
Both walk on across they look
The years those secrets hide
Then the mighty river grows
Across from you is me
A speck as last the river flows
Into the open sea

Raymond Peter Walker

What's A Panda Daddy

What's a panda daddy?
Well a long long time ago. They used to roam through China
They're all gone now, but why I just don't know
I think I read somewhere, pollution killed them off
But that was oh, so long ago. Before I got this cough

Are whales still swimming in the sea?
I think so but it's not clear, as poisons from the factories
Made many disappear
How can poisons from the factories, hurt fishes in the sea?
Well it's very complicated, and no one's quite explained to me

Well can you tell me daddy, are rainforests still around
At school our teacher wasn't sure, but in this book I found
It says a long long time ago, there were forests large and green
Filled with exotic birds and animals. And plants we've never seen
Where did they all go daddy? Is it true I'll never see
Real live moving animals. Like we see on TV

I saw a movie once. That spoke of acid rain
And it killed off nearly all the trees that never grew again
And the men dug up the forests, for the cities you see there
It seems the world's too small for us, and animals to share

Couldn't you stop them daddy? Didn't you even try
Did no one help the wildlife! Is the bible just a lie
God made the world for all of us, for man and beast to roam
Surely he would never mean for us to take their home
There was nothing much that I could do. That's why politicians
Talk
Come on baby, put your face mask on, and let's go for a walk

Don Woods

Judgements

He who judges, judges, judges.
To look at the Eucharist and say
'There is Christ,' is pure faith
For the angels have their places
Turning not a stone but a wing
'Tis ye your estranged faces
Miss the many splendoured thing
Satan and his armies tremble
When the least child
On his knees prays
      Bow down before the host
      Bow down before the host
      Bow down before the host
      Herein lies pure devotion

Cavan Mulvihill

Hills Of Home

When I saw the Malvern Hills
    I was just a child,
Lost in wonder as I gazed
    Hillsides green and wild,
Many years I roamed afar
    In city and in town,
Never did my heart forget
    Hills so green and brown.

In my dreams they came to me
    In every season fair,
Outline of the lonely hills
    Towering high and bare,
As the years were passing by
    Now I was fully grown,
To the hills I came at last
    They are now my own.

Roaming in the hills each day
    Fair or stormy weather.
Solitude I came to seek
    Treading turf and heather,
Wandering over meadowland
    Malvern Hills rise sheer,
Every shadow, cleft of rock,
    Every outline clear.

Often when amidst the hills
    In stillness and in calm,
Here where I forget myself
    Finding peace and balm,
Hills reveal to me the way
    Along the path of life,
In the silence speaks a voice
    Far from angry strife.

When a child I loved the hills
    Leaving memories deep,
What I glimpsed not understood
    I was still asleep,
Things intangible, unseen,
    Revealed in many ways,
I saw beauty in the hills
    Truth shone in life's maze.

Betty Mealand

The Day Before The Meteor Came

I lay back
Into my pastoral pillow
Following a green blade
To her breezy summit,
A slender tip
Waving afternoon to infinity
Dancing to a universe
Filled with more mysteries
Than ever crossed the hearts divide,
Occasionally a jet plane
Thundered across the airways
A pagan to miracle technology
Through centuries of wonder
I watched him become a fly
Upon a silver ridge of the cirrus sky
A sunspot against the smudge of our setting star,
All along the nova day
I observed our magnificent sun
Beacon from the horizons of forever
A silver speck
In another world's night
Elope into an ocean of delusion
Under stars beginning
To scatter the twinklin' confetti
That long since married
Old Father Time and Mother Earth
I suddenly wondered
If God was a lonely being?
With a thousand planets
Orbiting in a cosmic fingernail
When a shooting star
Rode across the night
Shining like a cigarette end

Of God-like dimensions
I felt exalted to be answered
By the meteoric thoughts
Of the extra celestial conjurer,

Paul C Reece

For You

'I give you my feet to do your walking;
My hands to do your work;
I give you my ears so I can hear you
Calling;
My eyes to do your looking,
I give you my voice to say I love you;
I give you my heart, for your own;
Most of all I give you my devotion.'

Alf Williams

Impression Of A Walk In Northumberland

Raindrops glitter on every gate,
and outline every fern and blade,
sparkling on cobweb, twig and leaf,
soaking hips and haws.
Puddles stand beside the lane
as still the fine rain softly falls.
Ivy, honeysuckle, moss,
cling on rocky walls.
Scattered by the freshening breeze
diamond drops splash from the trees.
Clouds veil all the distant hill
in a misty gauze.
Damp the rosebay willow-herb
and the heather on the verge.
And from tall and distant firs
a lone voice calls.

Dinah Pickersgill

Ode To The Other Woman

The first thing that he said to you was 'Hello, what's your name?'
And now I fear his life will never be the same.
Can framing words to him, of anguish and regret
Erase the empty nights, remaining empty yet?
Penned platitudes in sycophantic verse
Have only made the evil in you worse.
Will they undo the shattered lives you leave behind,
The withered body and the frozen mind?
Give back once more the father of the child,
Restore the goodness to that young love now despoiled?
Can you rest easy in your bed at night -
Does retribution offer you no fright?
How does your husband's love fit, now your lover's gone -
By your own doing - and you feel no wrong.
What hypocrite you are, are bare-faced liar.
You stole another's love, wreaked misery drear and dire,
And yet can still, warm suckling-up in bed
With him both wedded and unwed,
And thinking nothing of the child that you have bred yourself,
Thinking only of yourself, and self, and self.
A marriage broken now lies devastated,
Whilst you, the other woman, will stay Hated.

Corrie Francis

Ancient Sun

mile after mile,
the lone son of the ancient Kingdom,
rides on waves of confusion, thru tunnels
of hate, born from anger and deception
he strides
trying to escape the kingdom
and blast into
the ancient sun . . .

Robert Gallant (19)

Nostalgia, True Or False

Those long golden days of summer
When each morning was brand new.
The grass in the garden still glistening
Heavy with silver dew.

The plans we made, the games we played,
No terror and no strife.
Is this nostalgia talking
Is it true to life?

Our youthful days were endless
We thought we'd never grow old,
If we could hold time in a bottle
And in our hands just hold.

Would we see it as it really was,
Was it all we can remember?
All that remains of our youthful days
Is only a dying ember.

Isabel McEwing

Dragon's Blood

I tell the children stories, of how after dark.
When I walk my dog Benson, round the local park.
Magic occurs and Benson's coat turns white.
A horse he turns into, with me in armour bright.
We fight a local dragon, with hot and fiery breath.
But only fight till wounded, not until the death.
For I am after dragon's blood, it's magical it seems.
If drunk makes children healthy and gives them happy dreams.
I tell them how we charge, lead him a merry dance.
Getting in close, to thrust at him with lance.
How he in turn dodges, slashes at me with claws.
While breathing fire between, the most ferocious roars.
How he will suddenly rear, and smite at me with tail.
Which Benson my trusty steed, leaps over without fail.
The suddenly I'll dazzle him, with my shield so bright.
Dart in and wound him, thus ending the fight.
The children's mouths hang open, they look at me with awe.
'Anyone for dragon's blood?' In one voice comes back 'Cor.'
Now here is the secret, of what dragon's blood is.
Blackberry juice and lemonade, to give the drink some fizz.

Peter Madle

Whispering Voices

When the time comes, to pack up my things
and set sail over mountains and seas
I'm going to walk out the door,
you won't see me no more
Blown away like the leaves off the trees

And if I get lost in the shadows of the darkest hour
that's the way that it's going to be
I'm going to walk through the rain
across deserts and plains
Washed away like a shipwreck at sea

But memories still haunt me
and your love still taunts me
My mind is still full of confusion
mysteries and madness, laughter and sadness
Someone help me escape this delusion

Down the empty road at an aimless pace
I guess I'm just a loner at heart
But mile after mile, the call of the wild
tears us farther and farther apart

So I'll weather the storm
with my hands in my pockets
And my head looking down at the ground
whispering voices and faraway noises
Spinning me around and around
whispering voices are the only sound

But memories still haunt me
and your love still taunts me
Now my mind reaches out for seclusion
laughing and crying
Loving and dying
someone help me escape this intrusion.

David Newton

Cold Harbour Lane

Never go walking in Cold Harbour Lane,
And certainly not after dark.
If you're heading that way at the end of the day,
Take the longer route round by the park.

Night shadows come early on Cold Harbour Lane;
Best not be about when they fall.
Street lamps, which are few, with their pale, ghastly hue,
Cast strange shapes on the pavements and wall.

Then footsteps are heard along Cold Harbour Lane;
If you hear them, then hurry along.
If you linger, I fear, you are likely to hear
The sad, plaintive notes of a song.

For murder goes stalking in Cold Harbour Lane,
And sinister sounds fill the breeze;
Though no soul is about, you may hear the odd shout
And strange whispers that make your blood freeze.

Folks say long ago down in Cold Harbour Lane
A young captain was robbed of his life.
From a ship in the bay, he was making his way
Back home to his children and wife.

He sang as he strode along Cold Harbour Lane,
And laughed at the cold and the rain.
Death struck without warning, they found him next morning,
Lying dead with an axe through his brain.

There's still blood on the pavement in Cold Harbour Lane,
Blood that they say never dries,
And even by day, there are some folk who say
They can still hear the moans and the cries.

The blood that was spilled there in Cold Harbour Lane
Glimmers vivid and red on the stone,
Only terror and pain walk in Cold Harbour Lane,
So never go there on your own.

Norman Ford

Birds And Seasons

In spring.
Then brown flecked wings,
Outstretched in flight,
With eyes that shine like fiery rings.
And soars to thermal currents high,
He hovers seeking out his prey.
Then drops like stone on unsuspecting things,
About their business of the day.
The budding leaves and quiet breeze,
Echo the screams around the trees.

In summer.
The warm sun shines,
The summer day is still,
The road tar shines,
The haze distorts.
And yet above the music trills,
Upon the wing, soars and sings,
And yet was never taught.

In autumn.
A shot rings out,
The rooks go wild,
They lumber up,
And circle round.
The rain and drizzle stops them not,
They soar and glide a while and then,
Settle again, like falling leaves,
Coming to rest atop the trees.

In winter.
The sea is grey and flecked with white,
Across the road is blown the spray.
The crash of waves on rocky shores,
The day is dark as if 'twas night,
While over head in matching vain,
The black capped gulls with wings of grey,
Screams as they wheel and soar,
And beat against the driving rain.

Norman Wharry

Took With Them Memories

An island called St Kilda, Archipelago meeting you,
Scaling scree, barefooted locals.
Catching fresh fulmars, for stomach and warmth,
A false slip, they plunged into seas eternal.

Menfolk awaken, shaking hands with morning dew,
Discussing outside the days proceedings.
The famous St Kilda parliament,
Better than today's conglomeration of unbelief.

Sabbath observance, rightly important to them,
No electricity, no foolish frivolities.
Today holiness is trampled underfoot,
Like the used cigarette end, its use is finished.

Smallpox epidemic, no national health service rubbish,
Young, old evacuated like flocks of sheep.
Evacuation imminent, fresh environment awaited,
August nineteen thirty, set sail for morvern, Argyll.

Belongings hung, like picture frames hanging from
Haggard backs, tears mingled fresh expectations.
Leaving tilley lamp glowing, old in years,
The family bible, above bright hearth embers roasting.

Iain M Macleod

Painting A Creation

Canvas, lies like a blank white page,
paint! It cries as though in a rage.
Not quite so simple, you might say,
as you keep the anger at bay.

Amid the chaos, of thought; one interprets the vision,
disregarding any thoughts of a mission.
Putting charcoal to canvas, dissolves the anguish,
like water on fire, now to extinguish.

Concentration, comes into play
disregarding what others might say.
Giving vent to true expression,
is the object of the lesson.

Open-mindedness, requires inner-strength,
to go on at great length.
Then comes the sense of achievement;
on others' faces believement.

Realising, a creation,
is simply better, than any elation.

Alastair Buchanan

Regret

'Could I but have my days again'
'I'd do things otherwise.'
This wish is always made in vain,
The chance will ne'er arise.

'Tis folly of the barest kind
To live in retrospect.
That chance was there for you to find,
Blame none for your neglect.

That opportunity then lost
In life did change your way;
But whether to your gain or cost
Is something none can say.

That past events are clarified
To us in later years,
Is due (it cannot be denied)
To knowledge bought with tears.

Regrets are vain. 'Tis waste of time
To live thus in the past.
Today is here; the future's thine;
The end is coming fast.

Arouse yourself and cast away
Those visions of the past.
Exploit each chance and live each day
As if it were thy last.

B Harwood

The Garden

I have a secret garden with tranquillity replete,
With roses round about me and daisies at my feet
Forget me not, and violets, and bluebells grace the ground
While lilac bush and cherry tree their blossoms scatter round

It's peaceful in my garden, it's hedged around with prayer
Each time I pay a visit I find sweet solace there
The daisies bring me comfort, the roses proffer peace
Forget me nots to let me know that God's love does not cease

I visit in the morning as the fresh new day's begun
And again at even tide at the setting of the sun
The sweet dew of his presence rises pure with each new day
At sunset falling softly as the daylight fades away

Whenever you are troubled and your cross seems hard to bear
You to may have a garden to soothe away each care
As you dwell amongst its beauty refreshing peace you'll find
Just like my secret garden, you'll find it deep within your mind.

Priscilla Newman

A Nice Hot Bath

It is so refreshing to forget about work
To leave all your problems behind
And look forward to a nice hot bath
Where you can just relax and unwind.

With your whole body totally immersed
The water lapping below your face
You can escape and close your eyes
Oblivious of both time and place.

How heavenly to wallow and soak
Momentarily lost in a dream
Letting the cares of the world roll by
To disappear like the rising steam.

Enjoying a sense of comfort and pleasure
You could happily lie there for hours
To become cleansed and invigoratingly fresh
Due to its undoubted therapeutic powers.

A bath helps to relieve tension and stress
And soothe away every ache and pain
Until reluctantly you have to get out
And release the water to run down the drain.

B Hilditch

Guess Who Will Be To Blame?

I'm on a mission, but it seems impossible,
I've been told my views are totally illogical.
It's like trying to make a pound out of fifteen pence,
'Cos now my childhood views no longer make no sense.
The effect racism has had on society is extreme.
How can skin colour determine if someone is supreme?
There's a gap in our society and we need to fill it,
Give a knife to a white man and he'll stab you in the gullet.
All everyone wants is to live in prosperity.
I want this to, so why are you getting at me?
Black people are to damn lenient to the white race,
Most try to make us live in tortureful disgrace.
Keep us all in poverty areas.
Then we're called '*violent instigators!*'
We have role models in the wrong professions,
Time is running out, we should have now learnt our lesson.
We want black politicians and black political opinions,
We shouldn't be forced out like American Red Indians.
Blacks need to stick together so we can educate and change the
                                                    white man,
They want us dead because we're invading their beloved
                                                    America and England.
Have you noticed how Marcus was never in the news.
The white man wanted to cover up his potent views.
Unlike my predecessors, I will succeed my aim,
And if I don't *guess* who will be to blame?

Wayne Reid

Mortality

*(During an outbreak of cholera and gastro-enteritis in Delhi
- July, 1988)*

A dead sparrow lies in my garden
struck down untimely by callous fate.
Children die daily of cholera.
Every year thousands killed in earthquake, fire, and flood,
without a pause to think.
One step here, the next step - where?
No priest to guide the way.
No moment to prepare.
Just one step here, the next step there.
We are warned, 'Be ready.'
Know God here to know God there.
I haven't buried the sparrow yet,
my little messenger from God.

Jennifer Hashmi

Shine A Light

Send the light oh Lord across our dark land,
For the world you have control in your mighty hand,
It does not matter if we are, brown, black, yellow or white,
We are all precious oh Lord in your sight.

Send the light oh Lord, send it we pray,
Send the light oh Lord, send it today,
Save souls, and heal bodies too,
For there is nothing too hard for you to do.

So Shine Jesus oh Jesus Shine,
Until all the world are children of thine,
So send the light as bright as can be,
Until all the world turn unto thee.

So Shine oh Jesus all over our land,
For the world is in the palm of your hand,
Send the light oh Lord, oh send it now,
Till all the people oh Lord, At they feet humbly bow.

David Reynoldson

The Empty Bowl

Life seems at an end, before the end,
The cold grip of fear;
Fear of forever stopping,
Pity: humans don't hold life very dear.

Running around in circles,
Not thinking of dropping.
The cold grip on the soul,
From the day of consciousness,
Knowing there is an end:

Darkness, which is the seer,
So what if life is drear?
And humans are unthinking?
How does the problem solve itself?
How to prepare for that last sinking?
The last of good health,
Are we afraid of thinking?

Anna Parkhurst

Faces Of The Year

Spring's first morning, scintillating air
Earth's new growth with flowers in her hair
Young lambs leaping, frisking as they race
Thro' the meadows newly born,
That's her springtime face.

Sultry is the noontide, drowsy is the day
Bumble bees and butterflies pursue their painted way
Keen contented cattle, their verdant pastures pace
Awaiting evens solitude, behold her summer face.

Autumn evening, golden sky
Gilt-edged clouds that the wind throws by,
Pale blue vaults dressed in creamy lace
With fronds of gold, that's her autumn face.

Winter all encompassing, damp with mists and rain,
Diamond covered cobwebs deck the briars down the lane.
The watery sun tries valiantly the scudding clouds outpace
But all too soon 'tis dusk again, behold that's winter's face.

Norma Christina Robson

The Icelands

It all looked cold and distant,
the ice-faced mountain scenery,
yet the sun turned it into colours
so beautiful to see.

Pink magenta, and purple rays
shimmer the mountain, in its play,
fanning over the mountain tops,
jewels of colour from every drop.

Rolling water, tumbling from way up high,
a waterfall seems to touch the sky,
reflexs each colour every hue,
the rainbow comes with the dew.

Forces of nature so pure and clean
in the wilderness, where few have been,
tall woodlands covered with snow
painted pink, from the sun's glow.

Yet white fox and hares too
run its surface on snow so new,
in this vastness they search the land,
survive the bleakness without man.

Crashing water bounds off heavy rock
tumbling so fast the earth to mock,
but silver fish dip and dive
from seabirds they wish to hide.

Will men come to destroy that land,
destroying the beauty by their hand,
or let nature stay in harmony
for the generations, who have yet to be.

Naomi Ruth Whiting

Hidden Agenda

What is seriously meant by this?
Or any other government
Who claim to know what is best
For me, you and the rest.
They forever try their best to disguise
Their double standards and their lies
And morally lecture to you and me
Tell us what we can both do and see.

Whether in the papers, on TV or radio
Surely, deep down we all must know
The stories they tell are not true
The truth is hidden from me and you.
So, question it all, here, now, today!
Though do it in a sane and sensible way
For sanity is something they must not take
Though they will try if we do not stay awake!

P J Gassner

The Gamekeeper

With measured tread
He strides across his patch
Pheasants to feed
And predators to catch.
Through misty air
His plaintive call is heard
Whistling to tempt
The distant hungry bird.
Reluctantly
They filter to the sound
Then eagerly
Peck pellets from the ground.
With gun in hand
Through long wet grass he wades
Tending his traps
Concealed in woods or glades.
He does not rest,
He must protect his brood,
Know without doubt
That vermin are subdued.
He must ensure,
Among his other trials,
That he's aware
Of poachers and their wiles.
No harm must come
To any of his game
For if it does
Then *he* must take the blame.
He will patrol
Through daylight hours and dark.
Out late at night
And up before the lark.

Yet when at last
His long patrol is done
Forsaking them -
He drives them to the gun!

Joan Tompkins

Children In Rwanda

Write a poem for the children in this grief stricken, land,
Their face so empty their country so sad,
Victims of conflict they're calling to you,
So write a poem for the children, do what all we can do.

Save the children that struggle in the streets,
Poorest of the poor, begging to eat,
Living a life that's full of destruction,
In this grief sticken land hit by a famine.

Save the children, struggling to survive
Save their land, help them stay alive,
Save the children help them cope,
Stop a life of destruction give a life of hope.

Children of Rwanda, this poem is for you
We'll write these words and do what all we can do,
To stop famine, pollution, and common disease,
In your country so sad that's down on its knees.

Moose

Celebration

Disturbing air
Encroaching waves
Move through the tunnel to the drum
And ripple past
Mysterious caves
Of chalk and iron
Labyrinthine hum
Reach now the shore where pebbles gleam
And break into the dazzling stream.

Sparks from my tongue
Ignite and burn.
I catch your eye
And take my turn.
Together we lean back and stare;
Communicate
Disturbing air.

Jennifer Bell

For Children Lost

Angels tears now kiss the meadows
Reflecting in the new 'Spring light'.
The innocence of little children,
Their love still in our hearts locked tight.

Their beauty will - forever blossom,
Fuelled by the volumed strength of truth,
The gardens of our hearts replenished -
By the 'Budding' dreams of youth.

In candle glow - a realm of beauty -
A gentle calm bestills the night,
In the silence angels crying -
As from the darkness came forth light.

Malcolm Wilson Bucknall

Beauty

Words are beautiful,
As a smooth-flowing rivulet
Curves from its course
And rests its coolness
In shades and shadows,
Meandering forth
Into shining stretches
Of limpid light.
So does a slender skein
Of flowing words
Unwind across the conscious mind,
Weaving a spell
Of magic moments,
Formulating and fashioning the image,
The hazy gleam
Of a silver stream.
Smooth surfaces of thought,
Gathering and enfolding and extending
Into sequestered peace.
Lulled to form a harbour of fronding green,
Lingering long,
With olive, elongated finger
Probing into the furthest reaches
Of the river.
Forming a hidden haven
For restful, reptilian creatures
Framed in double-dappled sunrayed light.

Pettr Manson-Herrod

Asleep In God's Garden

Garden's beautifully laid out a picture for one's eyes.
Little pools and rushes all roofed by heaven's skies.
Mid these grounds there stands a tree of roses yellow hued,
Put there as its label says, for Mrs Evelyn Goode.
A brick chapel newly built, just where her ash was strewn,
Lit by the sun in day-time, at night time by the moon.
Opening wide the big glass doors, we softly went inside.
A pot of flowers in our hands we'd taken with such pride,
Standing by the wooden pew where one might kneel in prayer.
Books of service and of hymns were ready waiting there.
Altar hangings colourful yet modern in their style.
A lovely place to catch ones heart, to make one stay awhile.
Gazing round the chapel, standing by the simple bier,
Feeling people torn apart, had shed their grief in here.
Plants and flowers placed around by many loving hands.
Lovely colours, every hue, create a rainbow band.
Suddenly an empty spot held our glance, and so
Right there where her ashes fell we laid our gift to Ro.
Said a prayer, then both stood, with thoughts which rose above.
To the lady whom each day, we speak of with much love.
Then we gently closed the door, we knew our flowers would
                                                        bloom,
We know she is especially blessed. This is her private tomb.

Barbara Goode

A Boy On A Bike

A boy on a bike in a country lane,
Seen from the side of a passing train.
Ambling along, dreaming of what?
(Ah, that's his secret) - time forgot.

I don't know him; he doesn't see me,
But we're joined for a trice in eternity.
The afternoon sun is gliding the grass.
A moment in time - caught still - then we pass!

Margaret M Osoba

Crying On A Carousel Alone

Searching for existence in the puzzle that is me
I try to find reality; a reason just to be
Do I wear a smile today; do I wear a frown?
Shall I scream and shout today or shall I be a clown?

Will I have some purpose to take me through the day?
In this meaningless existence, will I find my way?
I want to show my anger; I want to show my pain
Yet when I try to be myself, I'm knocked down once again.

The maze of life's confusion leaves me right out on a limb
The search for true identity has made my vision dim
This crazy world we love to hate has left me standing still
There must be meaning somewhere this aching void to fill.

I need to search for answers but - where do I begin?
A creature of captivity securely bolted in
The people who are close to me may think that all is well
Is there a key to turn this lock - release me from my cell?

So - it's either on a soapbox or turn the other cheek
Would that make me strong as steel; would it make me weak?
Truth and confrontation might get me through the fight
But ships on alien courses float aimlessly through night.

There is one conflict left to choose; silence or speech
Both contained within my grasp yet simply out of reach
Silence shall be golden when truth alone is told
I will discard my mask today - risk it and be bold.

Judy Studd

A Shattered Peace

The birds all sang their lovely songs
As down the road I strolled along
Out for a walk all on my own;
It felt really good to be all alone.

What a lovely road to walk along
And with the birds join in song
While striding out all worry free
Down this road all lined with trees.

Into the fields leaving the road,
Through a stile in the fence I go.
It's here I could spend many hours
In the fields full of flowers.

Not a breath of wind in the air
When across my path ran a hare.
It seemed to travel ever so fast
Without stopping to see me aghast.

All of a sudden I got such a fright;
Along came a plane in low flight.
It screeched overhead shaking the earth
And left me shaking for all I was worth!

This spoiling my walk, I then turned around
And made my way back into the town.
If only our Government would take heed -
I'm sure this noise we do not need!

Francis Allen

Autumn

Mellow days and misty mornings,
chilly nights with stars so bright
tell us of the summer's passing.
Autumn's here but winter might
be still a full half year away.

Sunshine still has warmth to nourish
fruits and flowers, as each new day
sees the ripening of the harvest -
some for man but plenty left
for animals to take away.

As the dew in sunlight glistens
on a cobweb's silken sheen,
birds and animals are searching
for their food. I see them glean
all they need from trees and bushes,
grass and soil - a busy scene.

There is beauty in the springtime -
all is new and fresh and green
but the tints of autumn's splendour
pale the months which pass between.
As the year is slowly ending
nature's richest crown is seen.

Muriel Woolven

Holocaust

Ring out church bells,
Let your voices echo,
Through the barren streets.

Ring out church bells,
In memory of the dead,
And those who lie dying.

Ring out church bells,
Swayed by the wind of destruction,
For there are no men to ring thee.

Mark Cobbold

Is There God?

Is there a God I question, is there a God, I ask.
The world is in a turmoil and all man does is fight.
They fight against each other, no thought of the innocent's plight,
They die of disease and starvation, man seems to think that's
alright.

They want cars that go faster and faster, pollute the air with their
fumes.
He ruins the ozone layer, and makes disease rampant on earth.
Man only seems to cause chaos with his atom and hydrogen
bombs,
But no one cares anymore what they do.

If there is a God, why does He let it happen?
The world was so good that He made.
Man's greed for power is a disaster,
They don't seem to care as they should.

Power and more power is their objective,
But there is a power far stronger than man.
You've only to look at the seas for a start,
Man can't stop them flowing however he tries.

Man may think he is clever, but he's not clever enough.
He'll never control the weather, nor will he rule the skies.
Look at the stars in the heavens, the sun and moon in their
place.
The rainbow with its bright colours, no human hand could define.

Look at a tiny baby, count all its fingers and toes.
See how it smiles when it's happy, watch how it quickly grows.
Look at the trees in the greenwood, look at the flowers in the
field,
Look at the lambs in the meadow, then tell me there is not a
God.

Joyce Smith

Norlei

Dark gypsy eyes and black, black hair
And beads a jangling everywhere.
Rings on fingers glisten in firelight.
On the bright painted caravan steps you see her
Sitting there, in bright red blouse and
Veils in summer breezes drifting.
'I'll tell your fortune pretty sir.'
Stay if you dare, as wood smoke curls
And curls into the air;
And gypsy music stirs your very soul
To dare.
Then packs of cards are laid and candles
Flicker and shadows seem to be demons
Dancing everywhere.
Crystals catch the light of dawn
The fox runs home and birds start to sing.
And all the world is lost and city life
Seems tame.
You take the reins of the big brown horse
And as in a dream, you sit on the front
Of the caravan and smoke a white clay pipe.
And dark eyes look into yours
And black, black hair falls like a waterfall
And beads a jangling everywhere.
While gypsy children are laughing and dancing
And old wrinkled men are grinning while
Making pegs.
The caravans go over the hill and all is still.
There's just a whisper in the breeze that says . . .
'I'll tell your fortune pretty sir?'

Jennifer M Trodd

Dalriada

Where white cockle-shell sand meets the blue of the sea.
The shimmering green is a wonder to see:
With purples and mauves gleaming through from the weed
Held fast to the rocks, scattered like seed
Under crystal clear water on gleaming white sand.
The variety of colour with bright clarity and depth,
To attempt a description would prove most inept.
The quiet rippling sound as the sea meets the shore
Carried in on the breeze and over the moor
Till it meets purple grandeur of mountains galore.
A sight when first seen, will remain evermore.

J E Lindsay

A Reason

If we could choose, would we leave earth
Are there greater things above and beyond
There are those of us young in our years
Are called, having done no wrong
Ask ourselves, how can it be
As we are summoned up above
Does our maker know what's best for us
As he takes us from the ones we love
What possible reason can there be
There is still much more to live for, to be
                              be happy and free
Love ones left behind, cannot find a reason for it all
Carrying earthly problems and awaiting their call
If the promised land is really there to behold
Time stands still for young and old
All are needed for heaven above
It holds no fear we will all find love
Heaven is a place in the sky out of our control
Our spirits can seek solace in a heavenly role
At destiny's end we will all live forever
Enjoying eternity and reunited together
While we are in transit we are tempted and fall
Heaven was created for loved ones like ours
Taken from us when not so much more like a child
We will always remember his sunny smile
Earth is just a staging post, a watering hole
A place to shelter, ponder, till we reach our final goal

Daisy Thompson

Ghost Train

Out of the dark,
into the light,
the ghost trains,
just gave me a fright.
Ghosts and ghouls,
and horrible bats,
hairy skulls,
and screeching cats
flashing lights,
outstretched arms,
spiders' webs,
sweaty palms.
Down a slope,
around a bend,
oh how I wish,
it was the end.
Screaming down,
the track we go,
clackstons sounds,
hooters blow.
Pop up banshees,
skeletons swing,
eerie voices,
werewolf thing.
Then at last,
we reach the end,
I will never go,
on that again.

W E Simpson

Golden Key

The trustful heart will surely find
  When irritants appear,
That turbulent distress of mind
  Is tranquillised with prayer.

That prayer becomes a barricade
  To worry, grief, or pain,
And makes restricting shadows fade
  From the dark domain.

That prayer will keep a dream aglow,
  And help to bring success
To any great attempt to grow
  In strength and loveliness.

William Price

Child Of Ireland

Our day will come, what crime is ours?
So speak the IRA.
Our day is now as loyalists,
You will not pass this way.

But I'm a child of Ireland,
And in your turmoil war and strife,
My heart yearns for children's needs,
The simple joys of life.

Because I am republican;
And cannot other be.
Because my love of Anglia,
Ireland I cannot see.

But I'm a child of Ireland,
And you both my parents be.
And when you walk this road of blood,
You also murder me.

Our day will come,
Our day is now;

Then when will my day be?
For I'm a child of Ireland;
And would as other children be.

W Hopkins

Remembrance - Peterborough 1941

The distant sky was red,
But not with sunset glow
Giving delight to shepherds. No -
London blazed.
And high-explosive bombs dropped death.
We stood in silence on the country road that day,
Looking across the beetroot fields
At Armageddon, ninety miles away.

Mary Curtis

Meddling Muddle

I started working with the wizard,
About five months ago.
At first I thought it was boring,
But now I don't think so.

At the beginning nothing happened,
I just had to sweep and clean,
I admit the wizard's clever,
But on the other hand he's mean.

He has a change-o-matic,
(It's a very big machine)
It's always making static,
(It can turn a pea into a bean)

I found a spell book the other day,
I read a page while a rope started to fray,
The rope was holding open the trap door,
It slammed shut, and you could hear the wizard shout and roar.

The wizard came out and went upstairs
He looked behind himself and started to glare
But halfway up he fell
And at that moment I was casting a spell

The wizard got up off the floor
Again he started to shout and roar
The wizard then started to disappear
His head disappeared slowly and so did his ears

I ran to the door very quickly
And ran all the way down the path
I wanted to get away from that house
And get into a nice warm bath.

Ciaran McBride (9)

The Prize

A school prize won years ago
Gathers dust in an old bookcase
An old lady sitting all alone
With sadness etched upon her face.

One day a neighbour comes to call
With her grandson by the hand
He prowls around and finds the book
And gently removes it from its stand.

Can I read to you he says out loud
I can read some every day
It's winter now, the days are cold
So I can't get out to play.

Each day he brings such pleasure
To an old lady, very frail
He reads of pirates and far off lands
And of ships blowing in full sail.

The old lady smiles as she remembers
When she held her prize with pride
Her parents looked on with pleasure
As they stood there side by side.

The little boy brought back memories
She's not alone anymore
She closes her eyes for her last long sleep
As death gently leads her to a far off shore.

A S Logan

Sad Song

It wears me out
Something pushing me,
My head's hurting thoughts,
Affectionate squeezes.
This boring life!

Ashamed of thoughts of lust,
I want to sleep forever.
Tiredness captures me
Sleep, enrapture me,
With bodies of thinking minds.

Hurting childhood memories,
Growing pains' mentality.

Windows watch me,
Neighbours see me.
Look at us and fade out.

Time rushes us to death.
In loneliness, mine, my, me.
I in a crowded room with empty people.
Talk to myself, talk to me
Touch my thoughts,
Caress my heart.
Let me live and love.
Swallowed in vanity,
Everlasting inhumanity.

Songs and sounds run in my blood.
I rise to their beat,
My eyes hear their words.
And dance,
Dance.
My sad song that longs to live,
Live in a soft guitar.
Strum to my thoughts
Fingers shout my words,
Tune fill my head.
All day, and at night
Sleep in my bed.

Kelly Young

Take Me Away From Me

Lord when I see my brother hungry, take me away from me,
    make me stop, share and listen, and understand his
                    plea.
Grant me love, joy and peace, take me away from me,
    patience, kindness and goodness, take me away from
                    me.
Modesty, self control and chastity, take me away from me,
    pride, covetness and lust will only separate me from
                    thee.
    Anger, gluttony, envoy and sloth, in the end will only
                    punish me.
So heavenly father, you who have so much love for me, by thy
                    grace,
    the comfort of the holy spirit will surely take me away
                    from me.
Father, son and Holy Ghost, you love for me come free,
    all that I have to do, is put my life in your trusting hands,
    then you will do the rest, and take me away from me.

Barry D'arcy

Prometheus Arisen

The sky is empty and blue,
The sunshine is cascading to the floor,
A breeze is rushing across the ground,
And the land is dry and parched.

Across the horizon grey is destroying the blue,
Better put the animals away and lock up the door,
All is quiet and then comes a crashing sound,
The clouds are now gathering with their backs arched,
Drip and drop and drip and drop then rain comes faster,
Full pelt now with all the power unleashed,
The crack of the thunder is right overhead,
And the lightning strikes undaunted hitting the trees,
People running for cover know their master,
The volatile nature as now increased,
Get under shelter or you'll end up dead,
The storm is changing direction by ninety degrees,
Heading for the ocean and over the sea,
The violence is receding over the town,
The sky is becoming clearer over the cinema,
And the sun it's returning to see what as been.

Everything is alright for my family and me,
The mess it's caused is stirring a moan,
The play has now finished at this arena,
Across the horizon that grey-black sheen.

Jonathan Simms

Good-Bye My Love

As he stood alone surveying the scene,
He thought of how his life might have been,
Life has been so good with his wife at his side,
For she had been so gentle and kind,
Her love had filled his very being,
It was a love so true that had warmed his heart.

It's hard to lose a wife - someone who has shared your life,
They say big men don't cry but oh dear God I know they do and
why,
Jess I have wept buckets over you,
Why you had to go I'll never know.

We were together for such a short while,
My dear, you made my life seem so worthwhile,
The day that you consented to be my wife,
I little knew how you would change my life,
You were like the breath of spring,
From being alone I now had you,
To help and guide me in the work I had to do.

I never realised how much I counted on you,
I am missing you so much no more will I feel your tender touch,
You were my wife and my best friend,
When you were ill you were so brave,
Shrugging off the pain, you didn't once complain,
Oh darling I was so proud of you.

I still can't believe that you are gone,
I talk to you at night and pretend that I am holding you tight,
Then say Good-night my love Good-night.

I'll never find a love like you again,
For you will always have a place in my heart.
But darling I know the time has come,
When I must let you go,
But I just wanted to let you know how much I loved you.

The time has come when I must get on with my life,
And I'll remember always that you were my darling wife,
I know in my heart that we will meet again some day,
Jess - these are the hardest words that I will ever have to say,
Good-bye my love Good-bye.

Terri Brant

Growing Old

Isn't it strange that as we grow old,
The memory is unable to retain and hold,
Yet events that happened way in the past
To every little detail, memory holds fast.

Our sight's not too good, and eyes grow weary.
Making the outlook, a little bleary.
We get hard of hearing, but too proud to say.
What we have realised day by day.
When we join our friends for a little chat,
We only catch snatches of this bit and that
So many elderly have pains and arthritis
And which of us doesn't have some kind of 'itis'
Our joints protest as we bend and kneel.
Just one of the many aches we feel
How fortunate we are, still able to cope,
With life's ups and downs, and never lose hope,
Like the creaking gate, we'll hang around.
There's plenty of life in us yet to be found.
Hearing aids and spectacles all come into use,
At our age of life it's expected, is the usual excuse.
We tell ourselves we're still quite sprightly
Buying clothes which hide our bulges unsightly.
Shopping trolleys and heat lamps add to the list
Where would we be if they didn't exist?
When pension books are allocated, it would be nice to receive
Another for spare parts, our aches and pains to relieve.

E Kathleen Jones

92

Aqua Alta (High Water)
(A sonnet on Venice)

Footloose and free, I flounced to the piazetta
Free from medical aid, 'flight' in high heels.
I found someone wrote 'black' on David of the logatta.
The 'Baptistery' mosaics are loveliest of all!
The 'Giants' of the Doge look whitely bare.
(Those ceilings look more lovely than before)
The view from the 'Balcony' is a glorious glance.
The prison made me want to scream and claw
My way out, via 'The Bridge of Sighs!'
The latter looked more gracious from the
'Bridge of Straw'. But people are like flies
In summer! So, I stood below - camera whirr
In that moment I loosed a foot into the sea
So green, so playful - the Basin wetted me!'

Sylvia Dixon Ward

Down Our Neck Of The Bottle

It's 'Unhappy hour' two til three at Sam's,
where the drinks are twice the price.
The clientele don't care though,
they just want to drink. The bar staff too.

Always empty shot glasses spot the bar,
behind them: a sad story and
enough excuses for the next round.
Raising their glass to toast self pity.

And in their drinking they do find the solace,
that well-meaning clichés don't have.
There's plenty more fish supping gin.
And what doesn't kill you, makes you stranger.

The juke box paused the 'our song' choices,
only a stagnant choke remained
from the barman hanging himself
from the ceiling fan above them.
All eyes up.
Heavy burden turning.
Time a naught.
Self pity put on hold.
But then the juke box started,
and again they returned to their drinking.

J Thornton

I've Just Remembered

I've just remembered Ruth and Ruby in a Portsmouth pub.
Ten years ago today? A century past?
At any rate, some time ago.

One night, at six o'clock, the pub's doors opened:
We marched in but they were there before.
Six matelots in rig we were - on duty to get pissed.
'Get the wets in Hookey!'
'Hey you don't know Ruby. Ruby this is Dave.'
'And *this* is Ruth!'

Old Ruby pulled her colleague off the bar,
Lifting her by her lank and lacquered hair.
Ruth's face was smudged and ugly,
And was not improved when Ruby smashed it back
Nose-first into the puddled slops of beer on the bar.
'The old tart's puggled - leave her be!'

We laughed, we drank, and we went back to sea.
And now I've just remembered that encounter years ago.

Where are you Ruth and Ruby now you're old?
The pub's closed down and we've all gone our ways.
Some of us have become 'respectable'.

And yet we laughed at Ruth:
We mocked you Ruby - afterwards;
We showed you disrespect and that was bad.
We cannot blame it on our youth and ignorance, not now.

If I'd the power I'd call back that time . . .
            that pub . . . that day.
But then what other words, what better things to say?
The truth is that life's gone and yet . . .

And yet I *do* remember Ruby and her friend,
The inebriate Ruth.
So that's a kind of immortality.
I've just remembered.

Dave Walker

To Be Ashamed

To never think of others
To never give a damn
To hide away in corners
To be ashamed
To be a man
To take all of the forest
To bring it to its knees
To pollute all of the rivers
To pollute all the seas
To destroy the ozone layer
To poison all the air
To never think of others
To never really care

Alan Green

Are We Alone In The Universe?

I looked up, to the sky one night
A bright new star shone there
A shimmering, sparkling light
That twinkled, in the warm night air
I often sit and wonder
Why, stars, shine so bright
Way out, in the blue yonder
Does someone polish them, at night
On other planets, Mars, or the Moon
Is there, alien life forms here?
Who knows, but we may, find out soon
With all this sophisticated gear,
I wonder, what they'd look like.
What greetings, would they bring
Would they have names, like John, or Mike
Would their leader, be a queen, or king
Are we, alone, in the universe
I would only hope and pray
If spacecraft, ever land on earth
I hope I live, to see that day.

Peter Edward Waines Briggs

The Fairies

The fairies in the grass
Lightening up the dew
Bring an ambience of freshness
Especially for me and you

The magical tireless workers
Who are mainly sight unseen
Are responsible for the universe
Looking so cared for and beautifully clean

Just look at a spider's web
Fresh in the morning air
The butterflies and the raindrops
Looked after by those who care

The sunbeams of great warmth
From the glowing ball in the sky
Kept golden and full of dance
Especially for you and I

So spare a thought for 'The Little Angels'
With their many different tasks to partake
Give them a smile and a word of thanks
For they are industrious for our soul's sake

For all they touch is for our feeding
To give us 'light' and 'abundance' from 'above'
So have awareness of 'their gentle presence'
And open your heart to their 'unconditional love'.

Jade Deacon

Tortoise

As slow as a tortoise depends on its mood
But it can out run somethings when seeking food.
The creatures I know have a liking for sedum
And if there is plenty it's what one would feed 'em.
You will not deter it if its mind is made up
It will persist until it has supped
But should you want it to be on the go
It's true to its name and will really go slow.
Whether concave or convex tells the girls from the boys
And unless there is sedum they both can annoy.
It hides in its shell if one gets too near
Unless there is sedum and then there's no fear,
Out shoots its head on a long crinkly neck
Then sedum plants it will very soon wreck.
As slow as a tortoise depends on its mood
Unless there is sedum around for its food.

D R Thomas

A Calculating Cat

The tom cat in the kitchen
Sat glaring at the fish.
Till the cook came up behind him
And hit him with a dish.

He said you ate my kippers
And I'm sure you ate my plaice.
And the cat just sat and stared at him
With a smug look on its face.

The old cat wasn't silly
He knew the cook was old.
So in his mind he hatched a scheme
So evil cruel and cold.

The cook had often hit him
For sitting on the table.
And often left him without food
Of which he was quite able.

Tom came in one rainy night
And sat up in the chair.
But the cook came in for supper
And kicked him out of there.

The cat was getting ready
To hatch his evil plan.
The time was drawing closer
To get this nasty man.

The cook had changed the kitchen
For to suit himself.
He'd moved the bacon slicer
Down off the topmost shelf.

He screwed it to the table
Which he thought was so much nicer.
He didn't see the cat's eyes gleam
When he saw the bacon slicer.

He never saw the cat creep by
Till he leapt upon his back.
The last thing he ever saw
Were his hands upon the mat.

They say that cats are cunning
And very crafty too.
So never starve your tabby cat
Or the next one could be you.

D Burns

Vows And Promises

You left me for a new love.
You broke my heart in two,
You also broke the vows we made,
When you promised to be true,
We went to school together
Sweethearts from the start
You did not care you went away
And left my broken heart
But then I found a new love
'Twas heaven from the start
You picked me up when I was down
And repaired my broken heart.
We are so very happy
You treat me like a queen
Now I can put the past away
As if it was a dream
Now we'll grow old together
We share our joy and sorrows
You'll be there for me I know
For the rest of our tomorrows
And when our days on earth are done
I pray we'll be together
I should hate to part from you
For we are joined forever.

Maureen Baxter

Alone Society

Alone again there's no-one home,
Not a postcard or a phone.
It's me again and I'm alone,
No-one to talk to, on my own.

I turn to speak and turn away,
Then think about tomorrow's day.
The four walls closed me in today,
There's no-one out there worth a say.

Alone again and it's a pain,
Some might think it's just a game.
The game called life and all its force,
Your strings being pulled by another source.

'Catch 22' situations in this life go round,
Listen close your heart pounds loud.
No money for food or pennies for life,
I can't even hear a nagging wife.

Alone again no-one to touch or feel,
Not even time can make that heal.
In my life the penny's dropped,
It feels so hopeless life should stop.

I wake up for tomorrow's world,
Memories of no special girl,
What in life is all this for,
Just shut them all out. Slam the door!

In another world life would be,
There'll be no money, individuality.
Selfish actors on this planet,
Wouldn't be computerised and called 'Janet',

What's a cashcard and what's a name,
When all of us share life the same.
Enjoying life the way it is,
Without destruction and homeless kids.

Without roads and fumes of cars,
Idolising washed-out TV stars.
In this life for now stand tall,
Even if you're alone in concrete walls.

Chris Powell

To Leo Rex ~ Not A Tame Lion

No power in all the space of night can tame
The Lion whose savannah is the sky,
Can capture or confine his starry frame
Or turn the solar path he paces by.
The Lion walks in splendour, like the Sun
That rises in the summer in his sign,
While under his celestial feet there run
The silent paws of his wild kin, and thine.
And who shall bend these hunters to his will?
Or tell them what to leave, and what to do?
The lions prowl their ancient ranges still,
And some go on four feet, and some on two.
What I most fear to lose, I will not bind:
All his I am I dare not make all mine.

R D Gardner

Feelings

Alone is a state of being, loneliness a state of mind,
Anger brings hurt to everyone, with calmness it can be kind,
Hate is a thing that should not be, and love a thing to treasure.
Sarcasm is the lowest wit. But jokes a form of pleasure.
Crying sometimes can bring relief. By smiles, all are affected.
Morbidity should be controlled. And laughter given its head.
Sadness hurts at all its levels. Happiness is God given.
Lies are things we all should avoid. Confession will get shriven.
Cowardice makes you feel useless. Bravery adrenaline,
Ugliness shows up in all forms. All beauty comes from within.
Apathy too lazy to care. Caring can bring you much joy
Depression can be a killer. But hope can be an envoy.
Shame can eat through all of your life. Honesty can bring you
                                                    hope.

Boredom is a waste, find things to do, busy is better to cope,
Resentment is a waster of time. Contentment brings well being.
Conceit and ego are no good, self worth is gratifying.
Arrogance, people will dismiss. Angelic is of angels.
Aloofness can leave you alone, openness can form channels,
Erotic excess can be bad, but sexiness can be fun,
All these feelings go through out lives, you decide what will
            Be done.

Nicolette Andrèa Thomas

The Voyage

In 82
with a black hearted crew
we set sail from Plymouth Sound,
down in the Azores
we stopped from stores
for we were American bound.

Now the cook that we had,
a big geordie lad,
could make nothing but pork and bean stew
after weeks of this stuff
things began to cut rough
and mutterings came from the crew.

Three weeks at sea
becalmed lay we
not a wind not a breath nor a breeze
and Cap'n McHogg
said 'Break out the grog
I'll get cook to make beef and salt peas.'

Well he tried to cook beef
but it all came to grief
the men were seething with hate,
it smelt something evil
was crawling with weevil
and a year past its own sell by days

One mouthful of swill
the whole ship took ill
they ran to the side for a spew
then a bloody great roller
tipped 'em all over
and that's the last I saw of the crew

So now there's just me
all alone at sea
but I'm still alive, so I'm blessed
think I'll swim for the shore
any never no more
sail this ship called the
Marie Celeste!

G Holland